Table of Contents

Faith Alone is Essential for Salvation

A Transformative Truth

Dr. Anthony J Johnson Jr.

PREPARED FOR

LIVING WORD FULL GOSPEL MINISTRY AND BIBLE COLLEGE

RICHLANDS, NC 28574

Statement of Confidentiality

This project, **Faith Alone is Essential for Salvation,** contains confidential materials. It is to be held in strictest confidence and not released to any individual or organization for any purpose other than for the verification of academic requirements for graduation and for evaluation and approval by external reviewers to ensure compliance with outcomes assessment criteria. I understand that the College will keep one copy for academic verification **and periodic examination by others interested in the subject or the format of such academic work.**

Anthony J Johnson Jr.
Date

Acknowledgments

The author expresses heartfelt gratitude to the Class of 2025, whose camaraderie, dedication, and shared pursuit of knowledge have made the past four years an enriching journey. Special thanks go to the Board Learner Team Members for their unwavering support and encouragement and for making the learning experience both enjoyable and invaluable. I also extend my sincere appreciation to the volunteer staff of the Doctor of Theology Program, whose dedication has significantly contributed to making this academic endeavor both meaningful and transformative.

This work is completed in honor of my father, the late Pastor Anthony James Johnson, whose legacy of faith and wisdom continues to inspire me. I am deeply grateful to my mother, Diane Christie, and my eldest son, Tyler A. Johnson, along with many other cherished family members whose unwavering love and encouragement have sustained me despite the miles that separate us. A special tribute is also due to my grandmother, the late Ruth (Rufio) Thomas, whose steadfast prayers, love, wisdom, and kindness have left an indelible mark on my heart and continue to guide me.

Above all, my deepest appreciation goes to my beloved wife, Tauzlynn I. Johnson, who has been my steadfast partner in this humbling achievement. Her love, patience, and unwavering support have been a pillar of strength throughout this journey. Finally, I give all glory and honor to my Lord and Savior, Jesus Christ, for without Him, I can do nothing.

Abstract

This thesis argues that faith alone (*sola fide*)—rather than the act of baptism—is the true cornerstone of salvation, a distinction underscored by the deliberate omission of baptism in key biblical passages emphasizing justification. Mark 16:16 states, *"He that believeth and is baptized shall be saved; but he that believeth not shall be damned,"* highlighting that condemnation is linked to unbelief, not the absence of baptism. This study contends that salvation is a gift of grace received through faith alone, supported by biblical doctrine, historical context, and theological debate.

Through biblical analysis, this paper defends *sola fide* by examining Ephesians 2:8-9, Romans 3:28, and Galatians 2:16, which affirm that salvation is granted by faith in Christ, independent of works or adherence to religious rites. These passages reinforce that righteousness before God is imputed through faith alone rather than achieved through human effort or sacramental participation.

From a historical perspective, this study demonstrates that *sola fide* has deep roots in early Christian teachings, was solidified during the Reformation, and continues to shape Protestant theology. The research highlights how Martin Luther, John Calvin, and other Reformers rejected sacramental justification, emphasizing that faith alone is the means of salvation. Despite theological disputes, this doctrine has remained central to Protestant identity.

From a theological standpoint, the debate over *sola fide* continues to be a major point of contention between Christian traditions. Protestant Reformers defended justification by faith alone against Catholic and Orthodox teachings that emphasize a synergy between faith, works, and sacraments. These doctrinal differences have led to enduring theological discussions on the relationship between faith, baptism, and salvation.

Furthermore, this research discusses the dilemma of ongoing theological debates over *sola fide*, considering the consequences of differing interpretations and the obstacles they present to Christian unity. It addresses legalism and self-righteousness, contrasting these with the biblical understanding of grace while also cautioning against antinomianism, which distorts *sola fide* as an excuse for moral laxity. The study also examines the modern ecumenical movement, exploring efforts to reconcile Protestant, Catholic, and Orthodox views on justification and the role of baptism in salvation.

Ultimately, this thesis reaffirms that faith in Christ alone is necessary and sufficient for salvation, challenging views that incorporate baptism as a salvific requirement. By integrating biblical exegesis, historical theology, and theological debate, this study upholds the Reformation principle of *sola fide* while acknowledging the ongoing discourse surrounding justification and Christian unity.

Chapter 1:
Introduction

Introduction

Salvation is the central tenet of the Christian faith, representing deliverance from sin and reconciliation with God. Across different Christian traditions, the means of attaining salvation has been a topic of significant theological debate. While all Christians agree that salvation is found in Christ, they differ on whether faith alone (*sola fide*) or faith accompanied by sacraments—particularly baptism—is necessary for justification before God. This distinction has shaped the doctrines of major Christian denominations and has been a defining issue since the early church.

The question of whether baptism is necessary for salvation has been contested throughout Christian history. Some traditions, including Roman Catholicism and Eastern Orthodoxy, argue that baptism is a sacramental act that imparts grace and initiates believers into the Christian life. They often cite passages such as John 3:5, which says, *"Unless one is born of water and the Spirit, he cannot enter the kingdom of God"* (*English Standard Version [ESV]*, 2008), as evidence that baptism plays a direct role in salvation.

In contrast, Protestant theology—particularly within Lutheran, Reformed, Evangelical, and Baptist traditions—argues that salvation is attained through faith in Christ alone, apart from any external rituals. Proponents of *sola fide* point to verses such as Ephesians 2:8-9, which state that salvation comes by grace through faith and not by works. Additionally, they emphasize the deliberate exclusion of baptism from key passages about salvation, arguing that if baptism were essential, it would have been explicitly mentioned alongside faith in these definitive texts.

One of the strongest arguments for faith alone being the true cornerstone of salvation is the deliberate exclusion of baptism in key biblical passages concerning justification and eternal life. Passages such as Romans 10:9-10, John 3:16, and Acts 16:30-31 stress belief in Jesus as the requirement for salvation; they make no mention of baptism. If baptism were necessary for salvation, its omission in such crucial texts would be inexplicable.

Additionally, the case of the thief on the cross in Luke 23:39-43 presents a compelling example. Jesus assured the repentant thief, *"Today you will be with me in paradise,"* despite the thief having no opportunity for baptism. This further supports the argument that faith, not baptism, is the determining factor in salvation.

This paper argues that faith alone, rather than the act of baptism, is the true cornerstone of salvation, a distinction emphasized by the deliberate exclusion of baptism in key biblical texts. While baptism is an important act of obedience and public declaration of faith, Scripture consistently presents salvation as a result of faith in Christ alone. By examining biblical evidence, historical church teachings, and theological perspectives, this paper demonstrates that justification before God is based solely on faith, apart from any external rituals or sacraments.

Statement of the Problem

Throughout Christian history, the relationship between faith and baptism in the process of salvation has been a subject of theological debate. While many traditions assert that baptism is a necessary component of salvation, others maintain that faith alone (*sola fide*) is the sole requirement for justification before God. This divergence in doctrine has led to varying interpretations of Scripture, differing church practices, and ongoing theological disputes.

A critical issue in this debate is the deliberate exclusion of baptism in key biblical passages that explicitly define the means of salvation. If baptism were essential for salvation, one would expect its inclusion alongside faith in such foundational texts as John 3:16, Romans 10:9-10, and Acts 16:30-31. However, these and other passages consistently emphasize faith as the determining factor in salvation, raising the question of whether baptism is a symbolic act of obedience rather than a salvific requirement.

Purpose of the Study

This study seeks to address the theological, biblical, and historical implications of the cornerstone requirement for salvation by examining:

1. The biblical foundation for *sola fide* and the absence of baptism in key salvation passages.
2. The historical development of baptism as a sacrament and its role in different Christian traditions.
3. The theological consequences of requiring baptism for salvation and how it aligns with the doctrine of grace.

By addressing these concerns, this paper aims to clarify the role of baptism in salvation and affirm that faith alone is the true cornerstone of Christian justification.

Significance of Study

This study holds theological, doctrinal, and practical significance, particularly for scholars, church leaders, and believers seeking clarity on the role of faith and baptism in salvation. By critically analyzing biblical evidence, historical perspectives, and theological arguments, this study provides a well-rounded understanding of the doctrine of *sola fide* and its implications for Christian faith and practice.

Theological Significance

The theological significance of this study contributes to the broader discussion of salvation by reaffirming the biblical foundation of justification by faith alone. Emphasizing the deliberate exclusion of baptism in key salvation passages strengthens the argument that faith, rather than any external act, is the determining factor in receiving God's grace. The study also engages with theological traditions that support baptism as necessary for salvation, critically examining their claims in light of Scripture.

Historical and Doctrinal Impact

This study explores how different Christian traditions—particularly Protestant, Catholic, and Orthodox—have understood and taught the relationship between faith and baptism. Tracing the historical development of baptismal theology sheds light on how interpretations have evolved over time. The study helps to clarify misunderstandings that have led to doctrinal divisions within Christianity, offering insight into why some traditions emphasize baptism as a sacrament while others see it as a symbolic act of obedience.

Practical Relevance for Believers and Church Leaders

For individual believers, this study provides assurance in the understanding that salvation is secured through faith in Christ alone, without dependence on external rituals. This can deepen one's confidence in God's grace and remove confusion regarding the necessity of baptism for justification. For pastors, theologians, and church leaders, the study offers a clear, scriptural basis for teaching salvation by faith alone while still recognizing the importance of baptism as an act of obedience rather than a prerequisite for salvation.

The study can also serve as an apologetic resource for engaging in discussions with those who hold differing views, equipping believers to articulate the biblical case for *sola fide* effectively. By addressing these theological, historical, and practical dimensions, this study not only clarifies a foundational Christian doctrine but also strengthens the faith of individuals and contributes to meaningful theological discourse.

Definition of Terms

To provide clarity and consistency in this study, the following key terms are defined based on biblical, theological, and historical perspectives.

Faith: Faith, in Christian theology, refers to a confident trust and reliance on God, particularly in His promises of salvation through Jesus Christ. The Bible defines faith as "the assurance of things hoped for, the conviction of things not seen" (*English Standard Version [ESV]*, Hebrews 11:1). The Protestant Reformation emphasized *sola fide* (faith alone), asserting that salvation comes through faith in Christ rather than through works or rituals (Ephesians 2:8-9). Faith involves intellectual belief, personal trust, and obedience to God's will (Romans 10:9-10).

Baptism: Baptism is a Christian sacrament or ordinance that signifies spiritual cleansing, initiation into the Church, and identification with Christ's death, burial, and resurrection (Romans 6:3-4). Different Christian traditions interpret baptism in various ways:

- Sacramental View: In Roman Catholicism and Eastern Orthodoxy, baptism is a means of grace, necessary for the remission of sins and spiritual rebirth (Catechism of the Catholic Church, 1213).
- Symbolic View: Many Protestant traditions, particularly Evangelical and Baptist churches, regard baptism as an outward declaration of inward faith, signifying obedience rather than effecting salvation.
- Covenantal View: Some Reformed and Presbyterian traditions practice infant baptism, viewing it as a sign of God's covenant, akin to Old Testament circumcision (Colossians 2:11-12).

Salvation: Salvation is the deliverance from sin and its consequences, granted by God through faith in Jesus Christ. It is a central Christian doctrine, understood as a gift of grace rather than a result of human effort (Ephesians 2:8-9). Different theological perspectives on salvation include:

- Justification by Faith Alone (*Sola Fide*): The Protestants believe salvation comes solely through faith in Christ's atoning work (Romans

3:28).

- Sacramental Salvation: The Catholic and Orthodox view that salvation is mediated through faith and sacraments, including baptism and the Eucharist (John 3:5).
- Lordship Salvation vs. Free Grace Theology: Debates within Protestantism regarding whether genuine faith must be accompanied by works (James 2:17) or if faith alone, regardless of works, guarantees salvation.

By defining these terms, this study ensures a clearer understanding of their theological and doctrinal significance, particularly regarding the role of faith and baptism in salvation.

Limitations

One of the primary limitations of this study is the constraint of time, which affected the depth and scope of the research. Given the extensive theological, historical, and doctrinal discussions surrounding faith, baptism, and salvation, a comprehensive analysis of all perspectives is beyond the available timeframe. This limitation impacts several aspects of the study:

- Depth of Theological Exploration: While this paper examines major biblical and theological arguments concerning *sola fide* and baptism, it does not provide an exhaustive analysis of every theological tradition, particularly the nuanced differences within various Christian denominations.
- Historical Scope: The study focuses on key historical developments, such as the Reformation and early church practices, but due to time constraints, it does not delve deeply into lesser-known theological debates or regional variations in Christian history.
- Limited Engagement with Counterarguments: While opposing views regarding baptism's role in salvation are considered, the study may not have fully explored every counterargument in detail due to time limitations. A more extensive analysis would require additional research and scholarly engagement.
- Restricted Use of Sources: Given the limited time for research, the study primarily relies on widely recognized theological and biblical sources. A more in-depth study would involve a broader range of academic journal articles, historical documents, and theological treatises.
- Practical Implications: While this paper discusses the doctrinal significance of baptism in Christian life, it does not extensively explore contemporary pastoral or denominational practices regarding baptism, which could provide a more practical application of the theological findings.

Despite these limitations, the study provides a well-reasoned and biblically supported analysis of the role of faith and baptism in salvation. Future research could expand on these topics by incorporating more historical data, engaging with a wider range of theological sources, and conducting comparative analyses across Christian traditions.

Delimitations

Focus on the Doctrine of Faith Alone: This research specifically concentrates on the theological principle of *sola fide* (faith alone) as the basis of salvation, excluding a comprehensive analysis of other theological doctrines such as predestination, sanctification, or eschatology. While baptism is a key theme in this study, it is explored primarily in relation to its role in salvation, not as an isolated sacrament or in terms of its ecclesiastical significance across all Christian practices.

Exclusion of Non-Christian Perspectives: The research is limited to Christian theological perspectives, focusing primarily on Protestant, Roman Catholic, and Eastern Orthodox views of baptism and salvation. Non-Christian religious traditions and their views on salvation are not addressed in this paper, which is specifically concerned with the intersection of faith and baptism within the context of Christian doctrine.

Time Frame: The study is largely focused on the theological development of baptism and salvation from the early church to the Reformation era and does not engage in an in-depth analysis of more recent theological shifts post-Reformation, such as the rise of modern Pentecostal and Charismatic movements.

Exclusion of Denominational Practices: While various Christian denominations and their theological perspectives are discussed, this study does not delve deeply into the particular liturgical practices surrounding baptism in each denomination. Instead, it provides an overview of the theological underpinnings of these practices, focusing on the doctrinal distinction between faith as the means of salvation and baptism as an external sign or symbol of that faith.

Geographical Scope: The research does not specifically address the global spread of Christianity or how cultural contexts might influence the interpretation of baptism. The study remains focused on the historical and theological development of baptism within Western Christianity, particularly concerning the Protestant Reformation and its lasting effects.

Assumptions

This study is based on several key assumptions related to biblical interpretation, theological perspectives, historical context, practical and ecclesiastical implications, and methodological considerations. These assumptions shape the research approach and analysis of the relationship between faith, baptism, and salvation.

The following assumptions are made in the course of this research:

- Theological Continuity: It is assumed that there has been a consistent theological framework regarding salvation by faith alone that transcends historical contexts within Christianity. This assumption underpins the investigation into the development of the doctrine of *sola fide* and its application to the role of baptism in salvation.
- Reliability of Biblical Texts: The study assumes the reliability and authority of biblical texts as foundational sources for theological analysis. Key passages cited throughout the thesis, such as Ephesians 2:8-9, Romans 3:28, and John 3:16, are considered authentic and reflective of Christian doctrinal teachings on salvation.
- Historical Accuracy: The study assumes that historical accounts of early Christianity, the Reformation, and the development of baptismal theology are accurate as presented in widely accepted scholarly works and primary sources. It assumes the historical integrity of early church writings, Reformation documents, and ecclesiastical records that provide insight into the shifting views on baptism.
- Role of Faith in Salvation: It is assumed that the primary vehicle for salvation is faith alone, as espoused by key Reformation figures such as Martin Luther and John Calvin, and not by works or rituals such as baptism. This assumption is the foundation for exploring the relationship between faith and baptism in Christian theology.
- Ecumenical Diversity: The study assumes that different Christian traditions—Roman Catholic, Eastern Orthodox, Protestant—offer diverse but coherent theological perspectives on baptism and salvation and that these perspectives can be compared and contrasted

meaningfully within the parameters of this research.

- Exclusion of External Influences: This study assumes that the theological development of baptism within Christianity is largely shaped by Christian theological discourse and historical contexts, excluding significant external philosophical, sociological, or cultural factors that may influence denominational practices of baptism.
- Faith as the Foundation for Baptismal Practice: It is assumed that for most Christian denominations, baptism is an outward symbol of the believer's inward faith and spiritual transformation. Although theological differences exist regarding its role, the assumption is that baptism is seen across denominations as a public declaration of the believer's faith.
- Cultural and Ecclesiastical Evolution: The study presumes that the understanding of baptism has evolved within specific cultural and ecclesiastical settings, with theological ideas shaping practices more than the reverse. This assumption helps contextualize the changes in baptismal practice from the early church to the Reformation and modern day.

These assumptions are made to ensure that the study remains focused on the theological, biblical, and historical aspects of the role of faith and baptism in salvation within the framework of traditional Christian doctrines.

The Hypothesis

This thesis posits that faith alone (*sola fide*), rather than the act of baptism, is the true cornerstone of salvation, as evidenced by key biblical passages that emphasize justification by faith apart from works. While baptism remains an important Christian practice, its omission from essential salvation statements in Scripture suggests that it functions as an outward testimony of faith rather than a salvific requirement. This study hypothesizes that:

Biblical Evidence Supports Faith Alone: Scriptural passages such as Ephesians 2:8-9, Romans 3:28, and John 3:16 explicitly affirm that salvation is attained through faith in Christ alone, with no mention of baptism as a requirement.

Theological Tradition Reinforces the Distinction: The Protestant Reformation's emphasis on *sola fide* was a response to sacramental views of salvation, reinforcing that baptism, while significant, is not necessary for justification.

Baptism Serves a Symbolic, Not Salvific, Role: The early Church and Reformation-era debates indicate that baptism, though a command of Christ, serves as a public declaration of faith rather than a means of receiving saving grace.

Theological Divergences Present Ecumenical Challenges: While Protestant traditions emphasize justification by faith alone, Catholicism and Eastern Orthodoxy maintain that baptism is instrumental in salvation, creating an ongoing theological division.

These hypotheses will be tested through a thorough examination of biblical texts, historical theological positions, and modern ecumenical perspectives to determine whether faith alone is the sole means of salvation or if baptism holds a necessary salvific function in Christian doctrine. These hypotheses were also tested via survey. See Appendix A

The Theological Questions

To further explore the role of faith and baptism in salvation, the following theological questions are considered:

Biblical Interpretation and Theology

- What does the Bible explicitly teach about the relationship between faith and baptism in salvation?
- Why do certain passages emphasize faith alone (John 3:16, Ephesians 2:8-9) while others mention baptism in connection with salvation (Mark 16:16, Acts 2:38)?
- How did the Apostle Paul's teachings on justification (Romans 3:28, Galatians 2:16) shape the doctrine of *sola fide*?

Historical and Doctrinal Perspectives

- How did the early church fathers view baptism in relation to salvation?
- How did the doctrine of *sola fide* develop during the Reformation, and how did Reformers such as Martin Luther and John Calvin interpret baptism in this context?
- How has the theological debate over baptism and faith evolved among different Christian traditions (e.g., Catholic, Orthodox, Protestant, and Evangelical)?

Practical and Ecclesiastical Implications

- If faith alone is sufficient for salvation, what is the role of baptism in the Christian life?
- Should baptism be considered necessary for church membership, even if it is not required for salvation?
- How do differing views on baptism impact Christian unity and interdenominational dialogue?

Philosophical and Theological Debates

- Does requiring baptism for salvation contradict the doctrine of grace as an unmerited gift of God (*Titus 3:5*)?
- How do passages like *James 2:17* ("faith without works is dead") influence the debate on faith, works, and baptism?
- Can a person be saved without baptism if they have genuine faith but are unable to be baptized (e.g., the thief on the cross in *Luke 23:42-43*)?

These theological questions will guide the analysis of biblical evidence, historical doctrines, and contemporary Christian perspectives to determine the proper role of baptism in relation to salvation.

Chapter 2:
Literature Review

Introduction

Since the Reformation, the doctrine of *sola fide*, or justification by faith alone, has been a defining principle of Protestant theology. This literature review examines scholarly perspectives, although not an exhaustive list, but rather a sample of the theological distinction between faith and sacramental acts, particularly baptism, in the process of salvation. By engaging with biblical, historical, and theological analyses, this section explores how various scholars and scriptural texts support the primacy of faith over ritual observances.

A key component of this review is the examination of biblical evidence that affirms justification by faith alone. Foundational passages such as Ephesians 2:8-9, "*[8]For by grace are ye saved through faith; and that not of yourselves: it is the gift of God: [9]Not of works, lest any man should boast*" (*King James Version [KJV]* 2017) and Romans 3:28, "*Therefore we conclude that a man is justified by faith without the deeds of the law*" reinforce the theological position that salvation is granted through faith, not by external rites such as baptism. Galatians 2:16 and John 3:16 further emphasize belief in Christ as the sole requirement for salvation, distinguishing faith from any sacramental obligation.

Beyond scriptural evidence, this review engages with historical developments, particularly the Reformation's rejection of baptism as a salvific act, as examined by scholars like MacCulloch (2010). The theological debates surrounding the nature of faith, including critiques of alternative interpretations, such as Matthew Bates's *Allegiance Alone* framework, are also explored. Furthermore, works like Jonathan D. Watson's dissertation on baptism and catechesis provide insight into how ecclesiastical practices serve as responses to, rather than prerequisites for, saving faith.

By synthesizing biblical evidence, historical developments, and theological scholarship, this literature review establishes a foundation for the thesis that faith alone—not baptism or any other sacramental rite—is the true cornerstone of salvation. The analysis of key scriptural passages and scholarly perspectives underscores the enduring significance of *sola fide* in shaping Christian doctrine and practice.

Biblical Evidence for Salvation by Faith Alone

The doctrine of *sola fide,* or justification by faith alone, is deeply rooted in Scripture, where salvation is consistently presented as a gift of God's grace, received through faith rather than by human effort or sacramental observances. One of the clearest affirmations of this doctrine is in Ephesians 2:8-9, which states, *"For by grace are ye saved through faith; and that not of yourselves: it is the gift of God: Not of works, lest any man should boast."* This passage explicitly declares that salvation is granted through faith alone, emphasizing that it is "not of works"—excluding any human actions, including religious rites such as baptism, as a means of justification.

Similarly, Romans 3:28 reinforces this distinction by stating, *"Therefore we conclude that a man is justified by faith without the deeds of the law."* Paul's argument highlights that righteousness before God is obtained apart from legalistic or ritualistic observances, affirming that faith alone is sufficient for justification. This rejection of works-based salvation is central to the New Testament's teaching on grace and directly challenges the notion that baptism or any other religious act is necessary for salvation.

Furthermore, John 3:16, one of the most well-known verses in the Bible, supports this principle by stating, *"For God so loved the world, that he gave his only begotten Son, that whosoever believeth in him should not perish, but have everlasting life."* Notably, Jesus makes no mention of baptism or any other requirement beyond belief in Him for eternal life. This omission is significant, as it underscores the sufficiency of faith in Christ for salvation.

These passages collectively affirm that salvation is granted by God's grace through faith alone, apart from works or sacraments. They serve as the biblical foundation for the doctrine of *sola fide,* emphasizing that faith, rather than baptism or any other ritual, is the true cornerstone of salvation.

Scholarly Sampling Perspective Review

The thesis that *faith alone* is the true cornerstone of salvation—rather than the act of baptism—finds support and interaction with key perspectives in the works of scholars like Alec Ryrie, Hans Küng, A. N. Wilson, Henry Louis Gates Jr., Diarmaid MacCulloch, Rudolph W. Heinze, Richard A. Horsley, Gary L. W. Johnson, and others. Each of these scholars addresses aspects of Christian history, theology, and doctrine, providing varying perspectives that relate to the ongoing theological debate surrounding salvation, faith, and baptism. These perspectives illuminate the evolution of Christian thought on justification, salvation, and the role of baptism, offering insights that help frame and contextualize the argument that *sola fide* (faith alone) is the doctrinal foundation of salvation.

Küng's (1994) *Great Christian Thinkers* provides insight into the development of Christian thought across the centuries. Küng outlines the theological contributions of major figures such as Augustine, Thomas Aquinas, and Martin Luther, whose teachings emphasize the importance of grace and faith in salvation. Luther's doctrine of justification by faith alone, as articulated in Küng's text, played a central role in undermining the necessity of rituals like baptism for salvation.

In discussing the ecumenical movement, Küng critiques rigid doctrinal exclusivism and calls for reexamining traditional theological stances, including the role of faith and works in salvation. By advocating for a more inclusive understanding of Christian unity, Küng's perspective challenges the strict *sola fide* position, proposing a more cooperative theological framework. His work is essential for understanding the complexities of modern ecumenism and its implications for interdenominational discourse on salvation and justification. Küng's treatment of these thinkers underscores the centrality of *sola fide* in Protestant theology, thus supporting the thesis by emphasizing how the Protestant Reformers rejected the efficacy of baptism in achieving salvation.

Wilson (1997) explores Paul's theological insights in *Paul: The Mind of the Apostle*, revealing Paul's nuanced understanding of salvation, which places faith at the core of justification. Wilson argues that Paul's letters emphasize that righteousness is obtained through faith, not by works or external rites like circumcision (which parallels baptism in some theological contexts). Wilson's focus on Paul's teachings supports the thesis by illustrating that from the earliest Christian thought, salvation was understood as an act of divine grace received through faith, not through ritual acts.

Wilson argues further that while Paul did not create the Gospels, he played a crucial role in shaping the theological and doctrinal environment in which they developed. The Gospels emerged within a landscape of early Christian thought that was significantly influenced by Paul's teachings, particularly his emphasis on salvation by faith alone (*sola fide*) and the de-emphasis of Mosaic Law as a requirement for Gentile converts. Wilson asserts that Paul's theological framework—rooted in justification by faith apart from works—became a defining force in the early Christian movement, shaping the perspectives of the Gospel writers, even if indirectly.

Paul's influence is especially evident in the contrast between his epistles and the Jewish-Christian perspectives prevalent in early Christianity. His letters, particularly Romans and Galatians, forcefully argue that faith in Christ, rather than adherence to the Law or sacramental rites like circumcision or baptism, is the true means of salvation. This doctrinal emphasis created significant theological tensions, particularly with Jewish-Christian groups that saw baptism and adherence to the Law as essential components of the faith. These debates, in turn, influenced the Gospel accounts, reflecting both the Pauline emphasis on faith and the broader Jewish-Christian traditions.

Wilson's assertion that Paul "fermented" the controversial milieu in which the Gospels grew suggests that the Apostle's theological positions sparked debates that ultimately shaped the development of Christian doctrine. While the Gospels do not explicitly echo Paul's theological language, they reflect the struggles and tensions he addressed—particularly in how they present Jesus' teachings on faith, grace, and the Kingdom of God. This assertion aligns with the thesis of this research, which argues that salvation by faith alone was a central tenet of Paul's teachings and later became a cornerstone of Christian doctrine, influencing both the Reformation and contemporary theological debates on baptism and salvation.

In *The Black Church: This Is Our Story, This Is Our Song*, Gates (2021) focuses on the history and evolution of African American Christianity, highlighting how faith and salvation were central to the spiritual life of Black communities. An interesting note is that Landers says, In fact, records of Black Catholics – marriages, baptisms, burial registers – appear in the St. Augustine church records dating from 1594. While Gates' work is more focused on the role of the church in shaping cultural identity and resistance, it also touches on the significance of salvation through faith. In the section "Awakening and the Methodist Church," Gates describes the revivalist gatherings where conversions in those traditions did not require lengthy formal instructions, only inner communion with the Holy Spirit.

Gates also showcased a collection of portraits and photographs of preachers, evangelists, and missionaries who had shaped the Black Church since the eighteenth century, including Absolom Jones, George Liele, Richard Allen, Jarena Lee, Zilpha Elaw, Sojourner Truth, Garrison Fraizer, Frederick Douglas, Daniel Alexander Payne, John Jasper, Henry Highland Garnet, Julia A. J. Foote, Henry McNeal Turner, Charles Harrison Mason, Howard Thurman, Lillian Brooks Coffey, Martin Luther King, Sr, and many others. His discussion of the Black Church's theology supports the idea that faith—often in the face of suffering—remains the essential means of salvation. This perspective resonates with the thesis that *sola fide* is the cornerstone of salvation, transcending any external ritual.

MacCulloch's (2010) *Christianity: The First Three Thousand Years* provides a sweeping historical overview of Christianity. The period of context spans from A Millennium of Beginnings (1000 BCE) to the Culture Wars of the 1960s through to the beginning of the twenty-first century up to 2009. MacCulloch highlights the theological development of Christian doctrine, including the divergence between Protestant and Catholic views on salvation. He discusses how the Reformers, influenced by Paul's writings, argued that salvation could not be earned through rituals but was a gift received through faith. MacCulloch's exploration of the Reformation and its rejection of sacramental salvation supports the thesis by showing how the rejection of baptism as a salvific act was a central tenet of the Protestant Reformation.

MacCulloch highlights how rejecting baptism as a salvific act became a defining feature of the Reformation's break from Catholic sacramental theology. He explains that before the Reformation, the Catholic Church taught that baptism was essential for salvation, as it cleansed individuals of the original sin and marked their entry into the Christian faith. However, Reformers like Martin

Luther, John Calvin, and Huldrych Zwingli challenged this view by emphasizing *sola fide*—the belief that faith alone is sufficient for justification before God.

Although Luther retained the practice of baptism, he rejected the idea that it had any inherent salvific power apart from faith (MacCulloch, 2010). Luther argued that baptism was a sign of God's grace but not a requirement for salvation. Calvin distinguished further between the external rite and the inward grace it symbolized, insisting that salvation depended entirely on God's sovereign election and not on any sacramental act. Zwingli took an even more radical stance, viewing baptism as purely symbolic and rejecting any notion that it conferred divine grace. MacCulloch underscores that this shift was not merely a theological debate but a fundamental restructuring of Christian doctrine, leading to deep divisions between Protestant and Catholic traditions.

Through his historical analysis, MacCulloch illustrates how the Protestant Reformation redefined Christian initiation by moving away from sacramental efficacy (the power to produce an effect) and toward an understanding of salvation as rooted exclusively in faith. This rejection of baptism as a necessary means of grace distinguished Protestant theology from Catholicism and shaped the trajectory of Christian doctrine in the following centuries.

In *Reform and Conflict: From the Medieval World to the Wars of Religion*, Heinze (2005) explores the historical context of the Protestant Reformation, including the doctrinal disputes surrounding baptism and salvation. His review of major developments is illustrated by a timeline that spans from 1302 to 1666. Heinze describes the dramatic difference between the late Middle Ages society and modern European society as it relates to the all-encompassing role of the Christian church. Through this lens, he describes some origins, views, and practices of sacraments and their viewed role in answering the question, "What must I do to be saved?" From the Medieval Doctrine of Justification to leadership conflicts and various reformations over time, Heinze highlights the doctrinal clashes between Catholics and Protestants, particularly the Reformers' insistence on faith alone as the means of justification. Heinze's treatment of the theological and political conflicts surrounding the Reformation further supports the thesis by emphasizing how the Reformers' rejection of the necessity of baptism for salvation was a key issue in the development of Protestant doctrine.

In *Christian Origins*, Horsley (2005) examines the early Christian movement, including its roots in Jewish traditions and evolution into a distinct religion. Horsley emphasizes that the early Christian understanding of salvation, as conveyed through the letters of Paul, was rooted in faith in Christ, not in the observance of religious rituals. Horsley refers to Paul's letters several times as undisputed letters. He also notes that Paul received his gospel in a revelatory experience of the exalted Lord. Horsley's exploration of Christian origins and the teachings of Paul aligns with the thesis by underscoring that the foundational doctrine of Christianity was that faith, not external rites, was the key to salvation.

In the article "A Faith Unlike Abraham's: Matthew Bates on Salvation by Allegiance Alone," Timmins critically examines Matthew Bates's proposition that the New Testament term *pistis* (traditionally translated as "faith") should be understood as "allegiance" in contexts of salvation. Bates argues that this re-interpretation shifts the emphasis from mere belief to a committed loyalty to Jesus as the reigning king, suggesting that salvation is contingent upon this allegiance. Timmins engages with Bates's thesis by analyzing the lexical, theological, and exegetical foundations of translating *pistis* as "allegiance." He identifies significant deficiencies in Bates's argument across these areas, ultimately judging the proposal as untenable. Timmins's critique supports the traditional understanding that faith alone (*sola fide*), characterized by trust and belief in Christ, remains the cornerstone of salvation rather than a redefined concept of allegiance. Thus, this article does not adequately focus on the positional argument of this paper but contributes to the working definition of faith.

In the 2024 article, "Justification for Eternal Security of Believers and Impossibility of Apostasy in Romans 8:28-31," Inyaregh examines the theological concepts of eternal security and the impossibility of apostasy within the context of Romans 8:28-31. Utilizing a historical-critical methodology, Inyaregh analyzes the soteriological perspectives of Calvinism and Arminianism, focusing on how this passage supports the doctrine that believers cannot lose their salvation. He argues that the text emphasizes God's foreknowledge and predestination, suggesting that those whom God has called and justified are assured of glorification, thereby reinforcing the belief in eternal security. This interpretation aligns with the thesis that faith alone (*sola fide*) is the cornerstone of salvation, as it underscores the permanence of salvation granted through faith, independent of subsequent actions or potential apostasy. Note that the topic or concept described in the article as permanence of salvation is not in the scope of this research paper.

In the 2015 dissertation, *The Relationship Between Baptism, Catechesis, and Entrance to the Church: An Argument for a Theological Catalyst*, Watson examines the interconnected roles of baptism and catechesis in the initiation process into the Christian church. Watson presents a four-model framework that delineates various historical and theological perspectives on how these rites function as gateways to church membership. This framework offers a comprehensive understanding of the diverse practices and beliefs regarding initiation rites across different Christian traditions.

Watson's analysis highlights the theological significance of baptism and catechesis, emphasizing their roles in the believer's faith journey. In exploring these rites' doctrinal foundations, he underscores the importance of faith as the central element in the process of salvation and church entry. This focus aligns with the thesis that faith alone (*sola fide*) is the cornerstone of salvation, suggesting that while baptism and catechesis are vital practices, they nurture and affirm the faith that justifies and incorporates believers into the church community. Through his exploration of these models, Watson contributes to the ongoing theological discourse on the nature of faith and its relationship to ecclesiastical practices, reinforcing the primacy of faith in the believer's salvation and integration into the church.

Watson's contribution to the theological discourse on faith and ecclesiastical practices is significant because he critically examines the historical and doctrinal development of baptism and catechesis within the broader Christian tradition. His work underscores how different Christian communities have understood and applied these practices in relation to salvation and church membership. By presenting a framework that categorizes various approaches to initiation, Watson provides insight into the evolving role of baptism—not as a prerequisite for salvation but as a theological catalyst that affirms and strengthens faith.

Watson's research highlights how many Christian traditions, especially those influenced by the Reformation, shifted the emphasis away from sacramental efficacy toward the necessity of personal faith in salvation. He argues that while baptism and catechesis serve as important means of teaching and public profession, they do not confer salvific grace. Rather, these practices function as responses to an already existing faith that justifies the believer.

Furthermore, Watson engages with both historical and contemporary theological debates to reinforce the primacy of *sola fide*. He examines how early church fathers, medieval theologians, and Protestant Reformers navigated the relationship between faith and sacramental acts, showing that the trajectory of Christian thought has increasingly recognized faith as the fundamental requirement for salvation. His work also dialogues with modern ecclesiastical practices, addressing how contemporary churches balance the theological significance of baptism with the doctrine of justification by faith alone.

In doing so, Watson affirms the argument that salvation is attained solely through faith, with baptism and catechesis serving as outward signs of an inward transformation rather than as necessary steps toward justification. His scholarship thus provides a crucial perspective in reaffirming the theological foundation of *sola fide* while acknowledging the role of ecclesiastical traditions in the believer's spiritual journey.

Schreiner's (2015) *Faith Alone: The Doctrine of Justification* provides a comprehensive defense of the Reformation doctrine of *sola fide*, arguing that justification comes through faith alone in Christ apart from works. His work is particularly relevant to the ongoing theological debate over justification and the role of baptism in salvation, as it highlights key Protestant convictions while engaging critically with Catholic and Orthodox perspectives. This review explores Schreiner's argument and its historical grounding and implications for contemporary ecumenical dialogue.

Schreiner asserts that *sola fide* is at the heart of the Protestant Reformation, emphasizing that justification is a declarative act of God in which sinners are pronounced righteous based on Christ's righteousness, not personal merit. He traces this doctrine back to Martin Luther and John Calvin, demonstrating its biblical foundations in texts such as Romans 3:28 and Galatians 2:16. By emphasizing faith as the sole instrument of justification, Schreiner directly challenges theological traditions that ascribe a sacramental role to baptism in the process of salvation.

Schreiner critically examines the Catholic and Orthodox positions, which maintain that justification is both a declarative and transformative process involving faith, baptism, and works. He interacts with the Council of Trent's articulation of justification, particularly its insistence that faith must be accompanied by works and sacraments, including baptism. Schreiner argues that this position undermines the sufficiency of faith and the finished work of Christ, making justification a synergistic process rather than a monergistic (the theological doctrine that regeneration is exclusively the work of the Holy Spirit) act of divine grace.

A strength of Schreiner's work is his rigorous biblical exegesis. He provides detailed analyses of Pauline texts, contending that Paul consistently teaches justification by faith apart from works. He also addresses James 2:24, where James states that "a person is justified by works and not by faith alone." Schreiner reconciles this apparent contradiction by asserting that James speaks of faith's outward evidence rather than its instrumental role in justification. In doing so, he defends the Protestant interpretation of justification as forensic rather than intrinsic.

Schreiner acknowledges the need for theological dialogue between Protestant, Catholic, and Orthodox traditions but insists that *sola fide* remains a non-negotiable doctrine for evangelical theology. While he appreciates the growing efforts toward unity, he warns against compromising the core principle of justification by faith alone. His work, therefore, poses a challenge to contemporary ecumenism, which seeks common ground while grappling with deep doctrinal differences.

Trueman's (2017) *Grace Alone: Salvation as a Gift of God* explores the foundational Reformation doctrine that salvation is entirely a work of God's grace, independent of human effort or sacramental participation. He emphasizes that grace is unmerited and sovereign, aligning with *sola fide* by asserting that justification is received through faith alone, apart from works or rituals such as baptism. Trueman engages with historical theology, examining how figures like Augustine, Luther, and Calvin shaped the doctrine of grace in opposition to synergistic views of salvation. An example of this was captured when he highlights that "Warfield summed it well when he wrote, 'The Reformation, inwardly considered, was just the ultimate triumph of Augustine's doctrine of grace over Augustine's doctrine of the church.'" Trueman also critiques modern challenges to *sola gratia* (by grace alone), particularly from Catholic and New Perspective on Paul scholars. By reaffirming that salvation is initiated and completed by God's grace, Trueman's work strengthens the thesis that faith, not baptism or works, is the basis of justification.

Ryrie's (2017) *Protestants: The Faith That Made the Modern World* provides a historical and theological exploration of Protestantism's transformative impact, particularly emphasizing the doctrine of *sola fide* (faith alone). Ryrie argues that the Protestant Reformation was not only a theological movement but also a revolutionary force that reshaped global history. He underscores that *sola fide* was the defining doctrine that distinguished Protestantism from Catholicism, detailing how Martin Luther's theological breakthrough—rooted in passages like Romans 3:28 and Ephesians 2:8-9—challenged the Catholic teaching that faith and sacraments, including baptism, were necessary for salvation.

Ryrie describes that the Protestant movement was built on the conviction that salvation is a direct act of God's grace, received through faith apart from works or external rites. He examines how Protestantism redefined the role of baptism, shifting it from a sacrament necessary for salvation to an outward sign of faith. He asserts, "Real Protestants would understand how absolutely pervasive human sin was and would not pretend it could be tidied up with a little good behavior." This doctrinal stance directly supports the thesis that faith alone, rather than baptism, is the true foundation of salvation. Castillio shared a similar viewpoint as Luther, arguing, "I must be saved by my own faith and not in that of another."

Ryrie highlights how Protestant reformers like Luther, Calvin, and Zwingli rejected the Catholic view of baptism as a means of imparting grace. He describes Luther as an accidental revolutionary: " Luther's theology was not a doctrine; it was a love affair. Consuming love for God..." While Protestant reformers maintained the importance of baptism as an act of obedience, they denied its necessity for justification. Ryrie explains how this theological shift had profound consequences, liberating Christians from reliance on institutional sacraments and reinforcing the belief that salvation is an inward transformation through faith.

Ryrie also explores how Protestant traditions have maintained diverse views on baptism. While some, like Lutherans and Anglicans, retained infant baptism as a covenantal sign, others, such as Baptists and Anabaptists, insisted that baptism should follow a personal profession of faith. This aligns with the argument that baptism is a symbolic act rather than a prerequisite for salvation. Ryrie's analysis extends beyond the Reformation to examine how *sola fide* continues to shape Protestant thought today. He discusses how evangelical movements have maintained and even intensified the focus on personal faith in Christ as the sole requirement for salvation.

Johnson's (2007) *By Faith Alone: Answering the Challenges to the Doctrine of Justification* provides a strong defense for *sola fide*, addressing contemporary criticisms and reaffirming the doctrine's biblical and theological foundation. Johnson argues that justification is an act of divine grace received through faith alone, apart from works or sacramental observances such as baptism. His work supports the thesis by emphasizing that faith—not baptism or religious rituals—is the true cornerstone of salvation.

Based on the biblical foundation of *sola fide*, Johnson systematically examines scriptural evidence supporting *sola fide*, focusing on texts like Romans 3:28, *"For we maintain that a man is justified by faith apart from works of the law,"* and Ephesians 2:8-9, *"For by grace you have been saved through faith... not of works."* He asserts that these passages establish faith as the sole means of receiving salvation, countering arguments that baptism plays a necessary role.

Johnson places *sola fide* within its historical context, tracing its roots from early church teachings to the Reformation. He highlights how Luther and Calvin championed faith alone in response to medieval sacramental theology, which tied justification to participation in church-administered rites. Johnson demonstrates that Protestant theology has consistently upheld *sola fide* as the biblical doctrine of salvation, rejecting sacramentalism as a requirement for justification.

One of Johnson's best quotes on the historical defense of *sola fide* is: "The Reformers did not invent justification by faith alone; they rediscovered it. The doctrine was always present in Scripture, obscured by centuries of human tradition, until men like Luther and Calvin brought it back into the light." This quote encapsulates Johnson's argument that *sola fide* was not a theological innovation of the Reformation but a recovery of biblical truth. It reinforces the historical continuity of justification by faith alone, tracing its roots to the teachings of Paul while contrasting it with the sacramental system that had developed in medieval Catholicism.

Johnson emphasizes that *sola fide* provides believers with the assurance of salvation, as it removes reliance on external rituals and instead focuses on Christ's completed work. He warns against legalism, which adds works to justification, and antinomianism, which distorts faith as an excuse for moral laxity. His work encourages Christians to uphold faith alone while recognizing baptism as an act of obedience rather than a means of salvation.

Beza et al.'s (2023) *Justification by Faith Alone*, along with contributions from Amandus Polanus and Francis Turretin, offers a rigorous theological defense of *sola fide*, affirming that justification is based solely on faith in Christ, apart from works or sacramental rites such as baptism. Translated by Casey B. Carmichael, this volume provides insight into Reformed orthodoxy's stance on justification, aligning with the thesis that faith alone, rather than baptism, is the true foundation of salvation.

Beza et al. conducted a rigorous study of scripture and thus grounded their argument in Scripture, drawing heavily from key Pauline texts such as Romans 3:28, *"For we hold that one is justified by faith apart from works of the law"* and Galatians 2:16, *"A person is not justified by works of the law, but through faith in Jesus Christ."* They emphasize that justification is imputed righteousness—Christ's righteousness accounted to the believer through faith alone—rather than an infused righteousness conferred through sacramental participation. They also compare baptism to circumcision (Romans 4:11), arguing that just as Abraham was justified before receiving circumcision, believers are justified before baptism. This interpretation directly supports the thesis by reinforcing that baptism is not a requirement for salvation but a response to saving faith.

Additionally, they offer a theological analysis of the apparent tension between Paul and James on justification, demonstrating their doctrinal harmony by clarifying that Paul speaks of justification by faith apart from works (Romans 3:28), while James emphasizes that true faith is evidenced by works (James 2:24). Through this exegetical exercise, Beza et al. reaffirm that justification is by faith alone, while good works serve as its natural outgrowth rather than its foundation.

One of the primary arguments in this work is the rejection of sacramentalism—the belief that sacraments, including baptism, are necessary means of receiving justifying grace. Beza critiques the Roman Catholic doctrine that baptism is a prerequisite for justification, arguing that such a view compromises the sufficiency of Christ's atoning work. Francis Turretin expands on this by asserting that any attempt to combine faith with baptism as a requirement for salvation undermines *sola gratia* (grace alone) and distorts the biblical teaching that faith is the only instrument of justification.

This volume also traces the doctrine of justification by faith alone through church history, demonstrating its continuity from Augustine to the Reformation. Following John Calvin's theological trajectory, Beza et al. assert that the Reformers did not invent *sola fide* but rather recovered the biblical truth that had been obscured by medieval sacramental theology. Amandus Polanus highlights how early church fathers, despite developing sacramental traditions, affirmed justification as fundamentally based on faith in Christ. This historical perspective supports the thesis by reinforcing that Protestant theology's rejection of baptismal regeneration is not a novel innovation but a return to biblical doctrine.

The following statement by Beza encapsulates his firm stance on *sola fide*: "To mingle human merit with the grace of God is to overthrow the foundation of the Gospel; for if righteousness comes by works, then Christ has died in vain." This quote affirms that any attempt to combine human effort—whether through baptism, sacraments, or good works—with God's grace undermines the sufficiency of Christ's atonement. Beza particularly refuted the Council of Trent (1545–1563), which upheld that baptism is necessary for salvation. He saw this as a fundamental corruption of the gospel, reinforcing salvation as a divine decree rather than a sacramental process. As such, Beza conclusively argues against The Roman Catholic teaching on baptismal regeneration because it contradicts the sufficiency of Christ's atonement.

A key theme in Beza's work is the assurance of salvation, which he argues is secured through faith alone and not through continued participation in sacraments. When a sinner places faith in Christ, God declares them righteous, not made righteous through an infused grace as taught in Catholic theology. Unlike Catholic and Orthodox traditions, which view baptism as a means of imparting saving grace, Beza insists that justification is a completed act at the moment of faith. He warns against legalism, which ties salvation to human effort, and antinomianism, which misinterprets *sola fide* as a license to sin. Within his Thesis 33, he states, "We are justified from the first accusation by faith alone because only the righteousness of Christ seized by faith sets us free from the curse of the law." His balanced approach aligns with the thesis by emphasizing that faith alone justifies, but true faith produces obedience and transformation.

Sproul's (1997) edited volume, *Justification by Faith Alone: Affirming the Doctrine by Which the Church and the Individual Stands or Falls*, is a robust theological defense of *sola fide* and its centrality in Protestant doctrine. This work, featuring contributions from leading Reformed theologians, emphasizes that justification is by faith alone, apart from works or sacraments such as baptism. The collection reinforces the thesis by asserting that faith—not religious rituals—is the sole means of salvation, a doctrine that remains crucial for evangelical theology.

In addition to his support in the biblical and theological foundation of *sola fide*, a key focus of the book addresses Catholic and Orthodox teachings that link justification to baptism and sacraments. The contributors critique the Council of Trent's assertion that justification is conferred through baptism, arguing that this contradicts Paul's teachings on grace. They also challenge contemporary theological movements, such as the New Perspective on Paul, which blurs the line between faith and works in justification. The book reinforces that righteousness is imputed through faith alone, rejecting any view that makes baptism a requirement for salvation.

The book underscores Martin Luther's famous declaration that *sola fide* is "the article upon which the church stands or falls." The contributors demonstrate that the Reformers did not invent justification by faith alone but rediscovered its biblical truth, pushing back against the sacramental theology that had dominated medieval Christianity. This historical defense supports the thesis by showing that baptism was never biblically intended as a means of justification, only as a sign of faith.

The book also warns against the dangers of legalism, which adds requirements such as baptism for salvation, and antinomianism, which misuses *sola fide* to neglect Christian obedience. Instead, it presents faith alone as the biblical foundation for a transformed Christian life.

Conclusion of This Section

The scholarly perspectives reviewed in this study collectively reinforce the thesis that *sola fide*—faith alone—is the true cornerstone of salvation rather than the act of baptism. By examining biblical, historical, and theological arguments from scholars such as Alec Ryrie, Hans Küng, A. N. Wilson, Henry Louis Gates Jr., Diarmaid MacCulloch, Rudolph W. Heinze, Richard A. Horsley, Gary L. W. Johnson, R. C. Sproul, Thomas Schreiner, and Carl R. Trueman, this research has demonstrated the enduring significance of justification by faith alone in Christian thought.

From a biblical perspective, scholars like A. N. Wilson and Thomas Schreiner highlight how Paul's epistles, particularly in Romans, Galatians, and Ephesians, affirm that salvation is a gift of grace received through faith apart from works. Their analyses align with the Protestant argument that baptism, while an important ordinance, does not confer salvation but serves as a sign of an already justified believer.

From a historical perspective, scholars like Ryrie, MacCulloch, and Heinze provide insight into the doctrinal evolution of *sola fide*, particularly its development during the Reformation. They illustrate how Luther, Calvin, and Zwingli rejected sacramental efficacy and emphasized that justification comes by faith alone. MacCulloch and Heinze further demonstrate that the Reformers' rejection of baptism as a means of salvation was a defining moment in Protestant theology, distinguishing it from Catholic and Orthodox sacramental traditions.

From a theological and ecumenical perspective, the works of Hans Küng and Jonathan Watson explore the tensions between *sola fide* and the sacramental theology of baptism. Küng's discussion on the ecumenical movement highlights efforts to reconcile differences between Protestant, Catholic, and Orthodox views, while Watson's framework on baptism and catechesis affirms the primacy of faith in the believer's salvation. Similarly, R. C. Sproul and Gary L. W. Johnson defend *sola fide* against theological challenges, reaffirming that justification by faith alone remains the foundational principle of the gospel.

Beyond doctrinal analysis, the practical implications of this study emphasize how *sola fide* provides believers with assurance of salvation, liberating them from legalistic requirements while avoiding the dangers of antinomianism. As Gates' work on the Black Church illustrates, faith has remained a vital source of strength and salvation across various Christian traditions, transcending external rites and rituals.

In conclusion, this chapter affirms that justification by faith alone is not only a historical and theological conviction of the Protestant Reformation but a biblical truth with lasting implications for Christian belief and practice. While baptism remains a significant act of obedience and public profession of faith, it is faith in Christ—not baptism—that secures salvation. The ongoing theological debate underscores the need for continued dialogue among Christian traditions while remaining anchored in the scriptural foundation of *sola fide*.

These scholars provide a range of substantive perspectives that support the thesis that faith alone, rather than baptism, is the true cornerstone of salvation. From the Reformation's rejection of sacramental salvation to Paul's writings on justification by faith, these works highlight the centrality of *sola fide* in Christian doctrine and its enduring theological significance. Each scholar, in their own way, affirms the thesis by demonstrating the historical, theological, and biblical foundations of the doctrine that faith is the sole means by which individuals are justified before God while also affirming the necessity for maintaining the integrity of the gospel.

Chapter 3:
Methodology

44

Literature Review Process

The researcher conducted a comprehensive yet not exhaustive literature review utilizing diverse sources to ensure both historical accuracy and contemporary relevance. Primary resources included books obtained from the Onslow County Public Library, supplemented by additional scholarly works purchased on Amazon.com. Furthermore, to enhance the academic rigor of the study, the researcher accessed peer-reviewed journal articles and digital resources through the NC LIVE online database.

A deliberate effort was made to prioritize reputable, scholarly, and peer-reviewed sources that provide a well-rounded perspective on the theological and historical aspects of this study. The selection process emphasized materials that are both historically significant and reflective of current academic discussions, ensuring that the research remains relevant within the broader discourse on the doctrine of *sola fide* and its implications in Christian theology.

This literature review explores theological perspectives, biblical interpretations, historical developments, and contemporary scholarly discussions related to the thesis that faith alone, rather than the act of baptism, is the true cornerstone of salvation, as evidenced by the deliberate exclusion of baptism in key biblical texts on salvation.

Type of Research

In addition to the literature review, the researcher utilized a descriptive, exploratory, and mixed methodology approach to ascertain the varying positions that people have about *sola fide*. Thus, the researcher conducted a survey designed to collect data on Christian beliefs regarding salvation, justification by faith alone (*sola fide*), and the role of baptism.

Participants

The researcher primarily surveyed random people within one of the researcher's social media platforms. The survey invitation was also sent to some of the researcher's group text distributions, including a subset of a single church organization and a subset of bible college peers.

Design

The study collected independent responses via surveymonkey.com. The survey questions (Appendix A) were designed to capture the participants' understanding and/or belief regarding sola fide. The survey began with demographic questions, while the remaining parts captured participants' biblical understanding of salvation, theological and doctrinal perspectives, personal beliefs, and experience.

Procedure

The survey data was collected and systematically analyzed to identify trends, inconsistencies, and theological variations across different Christian traditions. The process involved the following steps:

1. Data Collection: Responses were gathered from participants representing various Christian denominations to assess beliefs about *sola fide*, baptism, and assurance of salvation.
2. Initial Trend Assessment: The collected data were reviewed for any immediate patterns or noticeable trends, such as denominational alignment with *sola fide* or differing views on baptism's role in salvation.

3. Outlier Identification: Responses that significantly deviate from the majority trends were analyzed separately to determine whether they reflect unique theological perspectives, misinterpretations, or inconsistencies.

4. Comparative Analysis: The data was evaluated in relation to doctrinal positions to determine if variations in belief systems highlight theological divisions and a lack of unity in how Christians understand assurance of salvation.

5. Support for the Thesis: Finally, the findings were assessed to determine whether the data supports the thesis that faith alone, rather than baptism, is the foundation of salvation. This involved comparing denominational responses and evaluating whether differences in doctrine impact how believers perceive their assurance of salvation.

This structured approach ensured that the survey effectively captured theological diversity and provided meaningful insights into the ongoing debate on *sola fide* and baptism. See Appendix B

Chapter 4:
Results

This chapter presents the study's findings, analyzing theological perspectives, historical developments, and biblical evidence related to the doctrine of *sola fide* (faith alone) and its implications for salvation. The results explore key doctrinal positions across Christian traditions, particularly examining Protestant, Catholic, and Orthodox views on justification and baptism. Additionally, this section evaluates how theological scholarship and scriptural analysis support or challenge the primacy of faith in salvation while considering the broader context of the ecumenical movement. The findings highlight efforts toward unity within the Christian faith, addressing both theological divisions and areas of convergence that contribute to ongoing dialogue in pursuit of greater doctrinal harmony.

Biblical Foundations of Salvation by Faith Alone

The doctrine of *sola fide* (faith alone) is deeply rooted in Scripture, particularly in the Pauline epistles. Paul's writings emphasize that justification before God comes through faith apart from works of the law (Romans 3:28, Ephesians 2:8-9). MacArthur (1995) argues that Paul's omission of baptism in salvation-centric passages suggests that faith is the sole requirement for justification. Similarly, Piper (2007) affirms that biblical salvation is based on trust in Christ rather than any external ritual, including baptism.

However, some scholars argue that certain verses, such as Mark 16:16 and Acts 2:38, imply a connection between baptism and salvation. Beasley-Murray (1962) contends that baptism, while not the cause of salvation, is an expected response to faith in the New Testament church. Nevertheless, proponents of *sola fide* maintain that baptism follows salvation rather than contributing to it (Acts 10:44-48).

The Role of Baptism in Early Christian Theology

Early church writings reflect diverse opinions on baptism's role in salvation. The Didache (c. 1st century) and Justin Martyr (2nd century) describe baptism as an essential practice but not necessarily as the means of justification. Augustine (4th century), however, developed the doctrine of baptismal regeneration, influencing Roman Catholic theology, which holds that baptism is necessary for the remission of original sin (Catechism of the Catholic Church, 1213).

Conversely, early Protestant Reformers, such as Martin Luther and John Calvin, rejected the necessity of baptism for justification, aligning with Paul's emphasis on faith. Luther (1520) acknowledged the importance of baptism but insisted that faith, not the sacrament, justified the believer. Calvin (1559) similarly argued in *Institutes of the Christian Religion* that baptism is a sign and seal of faith but not the means of salvation.

The Reformation and the Doctrine of Sola Fide

The Protestant Reformation was instrumental in solidifying the doctrine of *sola fide*, which became a defining principle of Reformed theology. Reformers rejected the Catholic teaching of baptismal regeneration, emphasizing that salvation is received through faith in Christ alone. The Westminster Confession of Faith (1647) affirms that justification is "by faith alone" and denies that baptism or any other sacrament contributes to salvation.

Scholars such as McGrath (1998) highlight how *sola fide* emerged as a response to medieval sacramental theology, reinforcing the distinction between justification and sanctification. While Lutheran and Reformed traditions continued to uphold the importance of baptism, they maintained that it was not essential for salvation. More recent scholars, such as Sproul (2014), continue to defend *sola fide*, arguing that the exclusion of baptism in salvation-related passages further supports the doctrine.

Contemporary Debates on Faith and Baptism

Modern theological debates continue to address the relationship between faith and baptism. Evangelical scholars, such as Grudem (1994), argue that baptism is an act of obedience but not a requirement for salvation. He emphasizes the case of the thief on the cross (Luke 23:42-43), who was saved without baptism, as a key biblical precedent for *sola fide*.

Conversely, Catholic and Orthodox theologians maintain that baptism is a necessary means of grace. The Catholic Catechism states that "baptism is necessary for salvation" but allows for exceptions such as *baptism of desire* (CCC 1257-1261). Eastern Orthodox theology similarly views baptism as part of the process of theosis (a Christian theological concept that describes the process of becoming like God or uniting with God), integrating faith and sacramental participation.

Recent studies also explore the impact of baptismal theology on church membership and Christian unity. Wright (2013) notes that while many Protestant denominations emphasize *sola fide*, they still require baptism for church membership, highlighting a distinction between justification and ecclesiastical practice.

Summary of Key Findings

The literature review reveals a longstanding debate on the role of baptism in salvation: Biblical evidence overwhelmingly supports faith as the means of justification, with baptism functioning as an act of obedience rather than a requirement for salvation.

Early church teachings varied, with some emphasizing baptism as an expected practice and others incorporating it into soteriology. The Reformation solidified *sola fide* as a foundational Protestant doctrine, rejecting baptism as a means of justification. Contemporary scholarship continues to affirm *sola fide* while acknowledging the ecclesiastical significance of baptism.

This literature review demonstrates that the exclusion of baptism in key salvation texts is not an oversight but a deliberate theological distinction, reinforcing the argument that faith alone is the true cornerstone of salvation.

Addressing Counterarguments

Baptism as an Act of Obedience, Not a Requirement for Salvation

In examining the role of baptism in the Christian faith, it is crucial to understand its purpose in light of scripture, especially in passages such as Matthew 28:19 and Acts 2:38. In Matthew 28:19, Jesus commands His disciples, saying, *"Go ye therefore, and teach all nations, baptizing them in the name of the Father, and of the Son, and of the Holy Ghost."* This passage presents baptism as an act of obedience and a command rather than a requirement for salvation. The focus is on the Great Commission, where baptism is part of making disciples and spreading the gospel message, not how salvation is attained. Similarly, in Acts 2:38, Peter urges the people, *"Repent, and be baptized every one of you in the name of Jesus Christ for the remission of sins, and ye shall receive the gift of the Holy Ghost."* While this verse links baptism with the remission of sins, it is important to understand this in the broader biblical context, where repentance and faith are emphasized as the essential prerequisites for salvation. Baptism here symbolizes repentance and the outward declaration of the inward change of heart, not the act that directly saves the individual.

Baptism, therefore, is better understood as an outward symbol of an inward faith. It is an important sacrament in the Christian life, serving as a public profession of the believer's faith in Christ. However, it is essential to distinguish between justification (the act of being declared righteous by God through faith) and sanctification (the ongoing process of Christian growth). Justification is a one-time event that occurs at the moment of faith, while sanctification is a continual process that follows as the believer matures in their relationship with Christ. Baptism is a part of the believer's initiation into the Christian faith, symbolizing the cleansing and transformation that occurs in justification, but it is not how salvation is obtained. In this light, baptism is an essential part of the Christian life, but faith alone brings about salvation.

Baptism has been a central rite in Christianity since the time of Christ, symbolizing initiation into the faith and a believer's identification with Jesus' death, burial, and resurrection. While theological perspectives on baptism differ among Christian traditions, its significance in the Christian life is universally recognized. The role of baptism can be understood through its biblical foundation, theological implications, historical developments, and practical applications in the life of believers.

1. Biblical Foundation of Baptism

Baptism is rooted in the teachings and practices of Jesus and the early church. Several key scriptures highlight its significance:

Jesus' Baptism and Command: Jesus Himself was baptized by John the Baptist (Matthew 3:13-17), setting an example for His followers. Before His ascension, Jesus commanded His disciples to baptize new believers in the name of the Father, the Son, and the Holy Spirit (Matthew 28:19-20).

Baptism in the Early Church: The Book of Acts records numerous instances of baptism following faith in Christ (Acts 2:38, Acts 8:12, Acts 16:30-33). Baptism was a public expression of one's commitment to Christ.

Pauline Theology on Baptism: The Apostle Paul taught that baptism symbolizes dying to sin and being raised to new life in Christ (Romans 6:3-4, Galatians 3:27). However, he also emphasized that salvation is by faith apart from works (Ephesians 2:8-9), which has led to theological debates regarding the necessity of baptism for salvation.

2. Theological Perspectives on Baptism

Christian traditions differ significantly in their interpretation of baptism's role in salvation and the believer's life. In traditions like Roman Catholicism, Eastern Orthodoxy, and some Protestant denominations, baptism is regarded as a sacrament that conveys grace and initiates individuals into the Christian faith. The Roman Catholic Church teaches that baptism cleanses original sin and is necessary for salvation, as outlined in the *Catechism of the Catholic Church* (1213-1216). Similarly, Eastern Orthodoxy views baptism as a means of participating in the divine life of Christ, emphasizing its spiritual significance as a transformative rite.

In contrast, evangelical, Baptist, and Reformed traditions typically adopt a symbolic view of baptism. In these traditions, baptism is not seen as a means of salvation but as an outward sign of an inward faith. The doctrine of *sola fide* (faith alone) is central to evangelical and Reformed theology, asserting that salvation is by faith alone, with baptism serving as a public declaration of that faith. Baptists, for example, practice believer's baptism, holding that only individuals who have consciously professed faith in Christ should be baptized. This view underscores the distinction between faith as the means of salvation and baptism as a symbol of that faith.

The covenantal view, held by some Reformed traditions such as Presbyterianism, involves the practice of infant baptism (paedobaptism). This perspective sees baptism as the New Testament counterpart to Old Testament circumcision, a sign of inclusion in the covenant community, as described in Colossians 2:11-12. While this view emphasizes the covenantal promises of God, it maintains that baptism does not regenerate the believer but signifies their membership in the community of faith.

Historical Development of Baptism

The practice and interpretation of baptism have evolved significantly throughout Christian history. In the early church (1st-3rd centuries), baptism was primarily by immersion and administered to new converts, with catechumenate programs designed to prepare candidates for baptism, which often took place on Easter Sunday. During the medieval period (4th-15th centuries), infant baptism became more dominant, largely influenced by Augustine's doctrine of original sin. Baptism was increasingly regarded as necessary for salvation, particularly in light of the belief that it cleansed individuals from sin.

The Reformation era (16th century) marked a pivotal shift in the understanding of baptism. The Protestant Reformers challenged the notion that baptism was necessary for salvation, leading to diverse views. Some Reformers, like Martin Luther, maintained a sacramental view, while others, such as Ulrich Zwingli, viewed baptism as symbolic. The Anabaptists rejected infant baptism altogether, advocating for believer's baptism as the only legitimate form of baptism. In the modern era (19th century to the present), many denominations have either reaffirmed or adapted their baptismal theology. Evangelicals, for instance, stress the importance of personal faith, while ecumenical dialogues have sought to find common ground on the meaning and practice of baptism.

The Practical Role of Baptism in Christian Life

Despite theological differences, baptism remains an essential practice in the Christian life. It is a public declaration of faith, symbolizing a believer's commitment to Christ and visibly identifying them with the Christian community. Baptism also represents spiritual transformation, symbolizing the believer's death to sin and resurrection to new life in Christ, as expressed in Romans 6:4. Furthermore, baptism is an act of obedience to Christ's command, as recorded in Matthew 28:19-20, even in traditions where it is not viewed as a requirement for salvation. Lastly, baptism is often seen as the formal act of incorporation into the church, signifying unity with other believers, as described in 1 Corinthians 12:13. Regardless of theological perspectives, baptism plays a pivotal role in a believer's spiritual journey, both as a symbol and as an expression of faith and obedience.

Baptism holds significant theological, historical, and spiritual meaning in the Christian life. While its role in salvation remains debated, it is universally regarded as a vital expression of faith, a mark of obedience, and a sign of belonging to the body of Christ. Whether viewed as a sacrament or a symbolic act, baptism continues to be a defining rite that shapes Christian identity and practice across denominations.

The Dilemma

There is an ongoing theological debate. The question of baptism's role in salvation continues to be a point of division between Christian traditions:

Protestant Views (Faith Alone)

Evangelical, Baptist, and Reformed traditions uphold *sola fide*, arguing that faith alone secures salvation and that baptism is an act of obedience rather than a requirement for justification. They emphasize scriptural passages where salvation is granted through faith without mentioning baptism (e.g., John 3:16, Romans 3:28).

Catholic and Orthodox Views (Faith and Baptism)

The Roman Catholic and Eastern Orthodox Churches continue to teach that baptism is essential for salvation, citing John 3:5, *"Unless one is born of water and the Spirit, he cannot enter the kingdom of God."* They argue that baptism is a means of receiving God's grace and entering into the Church.

Modern Ecumenical Perspectives

From a modern ecumenical perspective, the debate over *sola fide* (faith alone) and the role of baptism in salvation is not only a theological division but also a profound challenge to the unity of the Christian Church. As Christianity continues to evolve in global pluralism and denominational diversity, reconciling these doctrinal differences remains a central concern for ecumenical dialogues. The tension between Protestant, Catholic, and Orthodox views on faith and baptism illustrates how deep-rooted theological disagreements continue to shape the identity and mission of the Church in the contemporary world.

Protestant denominations, particularly those shaped by the Reformation, maintain *sola fide* as a foundational doctrine. The Reformers, most notably Martin Luther and John Calvin, emphasized that salvation is by grace alone, received through faith alone. For Protestants, the emphasis on individual faith as the means of salvation is central to their understanding of the gospel. This doctrine positions baptism as an important, yet secondary, practice that follows an individual's personal decision to place their faith in Christ. Baptism is viewed as an act of obedience, a public testimony of faith, rather than a sacrament that contributes to or secures salvation. For many Protestants, the notion that baptism is an essential component of salvation conflicts with their understanding of the sufficiency of Christ's work on the cross and the centrality of personal faith.

In contrast, Catholicism and Eastern Orthodoxy maintain a sacramental view of baptism, affirming that baptism is not only a symbolic act but also a necessary means of grace for salvation. The Catholic Church, drawing on centuries of tradition and theological reflection, teaches that baptism removes original sin and is essential for entering into the life of the Church. In the Eastern Orthodox tradition, baptism is viewed as a crucial moment in the believer's participation in the divine life of Christ. For both traditions, baptism is more than an outward sign; it is an effective means of grace that transforms the believer and initiates them into the covenant community of the Church. This sacramental understanding of baptism underscores a theological vision in which baptism and faith work in tandem for the believer's salvation.

In the context of modern ecumenism, these doctrinal differences present significant challenges to fostering unity. One of the most substantial hurdles is the difficulty in reconciling the Protestant emphasis on the sufficiency of faith with the Catholic and Orthodox teaching on the necessary role of baptism in salvation. For many ecumenical dialogues, this remains a point of contention because it touches not only on doctrinal beliefs but also on how salvation is understood and experienced within the life of the Church.

However, there have been some positive steps toward bridging these divides in recent years. One example is the 1999 Joint Declaration on the Doctrine of Justification, signed by the Lutheran World Federation and the Roman Catholic Church. While the document does not resolve all differences, it acknowledges that both traditions share a common understanding of justification as God's gift received by faith. Furthermore, the document primarily addresses the doctrine of justification; however, it has implications for discussions on *sola fide* and baptism, as it encourages a recognition of the role of both faith and sacrament in the salvation process.

Modern ecumenical efforts, while still acknowledging the theological differences, often seek to highlight the shared aspects of Christian faith and practice. Theological dialogues now tend to focus less on doctrinal differences and more on the shared beliefs about Christ, the necessity of grace, and the importance of community life in the Church. In this way, baptism, while still a point of theological distinction, can also be seen as a shared practice that signifies the believer's entry into the Church, regardless of whether it is viewed as a means of salvation or a symbol of faith.

However, while these dialogues have fostered a spirit of cooperation, the challenges in reconciling Protestant, Catholic, and Orthodox views on baptism and salvation persist. As the Church seeks to move toward greater unity, the ecumenical movement must continue navigating the complexities of these doctrinal differences while striving to preserve the integrity of each tradition's understanding of salvation. In this respect, the ongoing discussion about *sola fide* and baptism remains one of the most significant points of theological tension in modern Christianity, one that requires careful reflection, mutual respect, and a commitment to the unity of the Christian witness in the world.

Protestant and Evangelical Views on Baptism and Salvation

Following the Reformation's legacy, most Protestant and Evangelical traditions uphold *sola fide* and reject the notion that baptism is necessary for salvation. Scholars such as Grudem (1994) and Piper (2007) argue that while baptism is an important act of obedience, it is not a prerequisite for salvation, as evidenced by Paul's teachings in Ephesians 2:8-9 and the salvation of the thief on the cross (Luke 23:42-43). Many evangelical churches encourage believers to be baptized as an outward testimony of their faith, but they do not view baptism as effecting salvation.

Despite this, some Protestant denominations, such as Lutherans and certain branches of Reformed theology, hold a sacramental view of baptism, considering it a means of grace while still affirming *sola fide*. Luther (1520) saw baptism as a tangible assurance of God's promise of salvation but maintained that faith alone justifies the sinner. This nuanced position reflects the diversity of Protestant perspectives on baptism.

Catholic and Orthodox Perspectives: The Sacramental Necessity of Baptism

The Roman Catholic Church and Eastern Orthodox Church both teach that baptism is necessary for salvation, viewing it as a sacrament that washes away original sin and initiates the believer into the life of grace. The Catechism of the Catholic Church (CCC 1257) states: *"The Lord himself affirms that Baptism is necessary for salvation... The Church does not know of any means other than Baptism that assures entry into eternal beatitude."*

However, Catholic theology allows for exceptions, such as *baptism of desire* and *baptism of blood*, acknowledging that those who seek God in faith but are unable to receive baptism may still attain salvation. Eastern Orthodox theology similarly upholds the necessity of baptism but integrates it into a broader process of theosis (union with God), seeing baptism as the beginning of a lifelong journey of salvation rather than a singular moment of justification.

The Challenge of Ecumenical Dialogue

In efforts toward Christian unity, baptism remains a contentious issue. The World Council of Churches (WCC) and other ecumenical organizations have worked to bridge the theological divide by focusing on baptism as a shared Christian practice, even if its theological implications differ. The Baptism, Eucharist, and Ministry (BEM) document (1982), a significant ecumenical text produced by the WCC, sought to outline a common understanding of baptism as an essential rite of initiation into the Christian faith. However, while the document acknowledges differences in theological interpretations, it does not resolve the fundamental issue of whether baptism is necessary for salvation.

The dilemma remains: if *sola fide* is true, then baptism, while important, cannot be a requirement for salvation. On the other hand, if baptism is a necessary means of grace, then the Protestant emphasis on faith alone must be reconsidered. This theological divide affects not only doctrinal discussions but also practical issues such as interdenominational cooperation, church membership, and recognition of baptisms performed by different Christian traditions.

Practical Implications for Modern Christianity

- **Interdenominational Relations:** Many Protestant and Evangelical churches accept Catholic and Orthodox baptisms as valid, whereas Catholic and Orthodox traditions do not always recognize Protestant baptisms, particularly if they are not performed with a Trinitarian formula.

- **Church Membership and Sacramental Participation:** Some denominations require baptism for full membership, even if they do not see it as necessary for salvation. This creates a paradox where baptism is not theologically essential but is practically necessary for full participation in the church.

- **Christian Unity and Theological Consistency:** Efforts toward unity often require doctrinal compromise or a focus on shared beliefs while allowing theological diversity. The ongoing debate over baptism and *sola fide* highlights the challenge of maintaining biblical fidelity and ecumenical cooperation.

Conclusion of This Section

Throughout history, the doctrine of salvation has been shaped by biblical interpretation, theological evolution, and church tradition. While early Christianity valued baptism, the Reformation clarified that faith alone is the means of salvation. The deliberate exclusion of baptism in many key biblical passages further reinforces that faith—not ritual—is the foundation of salvation.

The modern ecumenical landscape reflects the ongoing tension between the doctrine of *sola fide* and sacramental views of baptism. While Protestants emphasize faith alone as the basis of salvation, Catholic and Orthodox traditions maintain the necessity of baptism as a means of grace. The debate continues to shape theological discussions, church practices, and efforts toward Christian unity. The question remains: Can a biblical and theological consensus be reached, or will baptism remain a defining point of division among Christian traditions?

Chapter 5:
Conclusions And Recommendations

Discussion

As stated in Chapter 4, the dilemma regarding the ongoing debate over *sola fide* (faith alone) and baptism remains a significant theological divide in Christianity. Protestants assert that justification is by faith alone, as supported by Ephesians 2:8-9 and Romans 3:28, rejecting the idea that sacraments contribute to salvation. In contrast, Catholic and Orthodox traditions view baptism as an essential means of grace, affirming its necessity for salvation (*Catechism of the Catholic Church*, 1257). This divergence creates a theological dilemma with implications for doctrine, church unity, and individual assurance of salvation.

Faith vs. Sacraments in Justification

The primary tension lies in whether salvation is solely by faith or if baptism is a necessary means of receiving grace. Protestants uphold *sola fide*, emphasizing that salvation is a gift received apart from works. Catholic and Orthodox traditions, however, integrate baptism into the salvation process, arguing that it confers divine grace and initiates believers into the Church (Acts 2:38). This fundamental difference shapes theological interpretations and ecclesiastical practices.

Impact on Christian Unity and Ecumenism

This doctrinal divide complicates ecumenical efforts. While agreements like the 1999 Joint Declaration on the Doctrine of Justification sought common ground, they failed to reconcile baptism's role in salvation. Differences in baptismal recognition further impact church membership, interdenominational cooperation, and sacramental participation, challenging unity among Christian traditions.

Assurance of Salvation and Practical Concerns

For Protestants, *sola fide* offers assurance of salvation through faith in Christ alone, without dependence on external rites. In contrast, Catholic and Orthodox traditions face theological challenges regarding unbaptized believers, relying on doctrines like *baptism of desire* to address concerns about salvation apart from baptism. This tension affects pastoral care, conversion practices, and Christian discipleship.

Biblical Challenges and Interpretative Differences

Both sides cite Scripture to defend their views. Protestants emphasize passages like John 3:16, which highlight belief as the sole requirement for eternal life. Meanwhile, Catholics and Orthodox point to verses like Acts 2:38 and James 2:24, arguing that faith and works—including baptism—play a role in salvation. Reconciling these perspectives remains a central biblical and theological challenge.

The Way Forward: Engaging with Tradition and Unity

Despite these differences, meaningful dialogue continues. Theological engagement must balance doctrinal conviction with a commitment to unity, recognizing baptism's significance even within traditions that reject its salvific necessity. Further, biblical scholarship and historical study may help bridge gaps, fostering deeper understanding while maintaining theological integrity.

Consequences of the Theological Dilemma

Theological Impact: The divide over justification and baptism sustains doctrinal differences between Protestant, Catholic, and Orthodox traditions. Key biblical texts (Ephesians 2:8-9, Romans 3:28, Acts 2:38) are interpreted differently, fueling ongoing disputes over grace, faith, and works.

Church and Ecumenical Challenges: Disagreements on baptism's role hinder interdenominational unity and create inconsistencies in church membership requirements. While ecumenical efforts like the 1999 Joint Declaration on Justification seek common ground, baptism remains a barrier to full reconciliation.

Practical Effects on Faith and Evangelism: Protestants find assurance in faith alone, while sacramental traditions emphasize baptism's necessity, leading to different approaches to salvation and discipleship. Misinterpretations of *sola fide* can either promote legalism or antinomianism, affecting Christian practice.

The debate over *sola fide* and baptism remains unresolved, shaping Christian theology, church practices, and ecumenical dialogue. While Protestant theology emphasizes faith alone, Catholic and Orthodox traditions affirm baptism's role in salvation, leading to doctrinal tensions that persist today. Engaging these theological differences with humility and scholarship is essential for greater unity in the Christian faith.

Proposals to Address The Dilemma

Encouraging Theological Dialogue and Ecumenical Cooperation

Greater unity requires open and respectful theological discourse between Protestant, Catholic, and Orthodox traditions. Existing efforts, such as the 1999 Joint Declaration on the Doctrine of Justification, have demonstrated that common ground can be found, even when doctrinal differences remain. Further ecumenical discussions should focus on shared beliefs—such as salvation through Christ, the authority of Scripture, and the importance of grace—while acknowledging theological distinctions with humility. Church leaders, scholars, and theologians should continue engaging in formal and informal dialogues that seek understanding rather than division.

Reaffirming the Primacy of Scripture in Theological Discussion

Since all Christian traditions regard the Bible as authoritative, greater unity can be achieved by grounding theological discussions in scriptural study. While interpretations of justification and baptism vary, a renewed focus on biblical exegesis—examining texts like Romans 3:28, Ephesians 2:8-9, Acts 2:38, and James 2:24—can clarify commonalities and areas of divergence. Joint theological commissions and interdenominational study groups can provide a platform for believers from different backgrounds to engage with Scripture together, fostering mutual understanding.

Recognizing the Spiritual and Communal Importance of Baptism

While theological disagreements persist regarding baptism's role in salvation, Christian traditions can find unity by emphasizing baptism's spiritual and communal significance. Even among those who do not see baptism as a requirement for salvation, it remains a public declaration of faith and a symbol of inclusion in the body of Christ. Protestant, Catholic, and Orthodox traditions should affirm the unifying role of baptism as an act of obedience and commitment to Christian life, even if its theological function differs across traditions.

Promoting Unity in Christian Practice and Mission

Despite doctrinal differences, Christians share a common mission: proclaiming the gospel, serving others, and living out the teachings of Christ. Churches from different backgrounds can collaborate in areas such as evangelism, social justice, humanitarian aid, and community outreach. When Christians work together in these areas, theological differences become secondary to their shared purpose of advancing God's kingdom. Encouraging interdenominational partnerships in missions and charitable work strengthens unity and reflects the love of Christ.

Avoiding Doctrinal Exclusivism and Emphasizing Core Christian Beliefs

Doctrinal exclusivism—where one tradition dismisses others as illegitimate—often hinders unity. Instead, Christian groups should acknowledge that while doctrinal distinctions matter, they do not negate shared faith in Jesus Christ. For example, the Apostles' Creed and Nicene Creed serve as unifying statements that encapsulate fundamental Christian beliefs. By affirming these core doctrines while allowing for respectful theological diversity, greater unity can be achieved without compromising essential truths.

Educating Believers on Theological Diversity with Grace and Humility

Many doctrinal disputes arise from misunderstanding or misrepresenting other traditions. Christian education programs, seminaries, and local churches should teach believers about theological diversity within Christianity, presenting different perspectives fairly and without bias. When believers are educated about various traditions with grace and humility, they are more likely to approach theological discussions with respect rather than hostility.

Conclusion

Achieving greater unity in the Christian faith requires a balance between theological conviction and mutual understanding. Christian traditions can move toward deeper unity by fostering dialogue, engaging with Scripture together, recognizing baptism's communal role, working collaboratively in Christian mission, and avoiding exclusivism. While differences in doctrine will always exist, a spirit of humility, love, and shared commitment to Christ can help bridge divides, allowing for a more unified and effective witness to the world.

This research was geared toward examining the theological debate surrounding *sola fide* (faith alone) and its implications for salvation, particularly regarding baptism. By analyzing biblical evidence, historical theological developments, and modern ecumenical perspectives, this study aimed to determine whether faith alone is the true cornerstone of salvation or if baptism is necessary in the justification process.

The study sought to:

Clarify the Biblical Basis for *Sola Fide*: By analyzing key scriptural passages such as Ephesians 2:8-9, Romans 3:28, and John 3:16, this research examined whether the Bible supports justification by faith alone or includes baptism as an essential requirement for salvation.

Compare Theological Perspectives Across Christian Traditions: This research explored how different Christian traditions—Protestant, Catholic, and Orthodox—interpret faith, baptism, and salvation. It investigated the Reformers' rejection of sacramental justification and contrasted it with the sacramental theology of Catholicism and Eastern Orthodoxy.

Examine the Historical Development of the Doctrine of Justification: By tracing how *sola fide* emerged as a central doctrine of the Reformation, this study evaluated how early church teachings, medieval theology, and Reformation-era debates shaped modern Christian understandings of salvation and baptism.

Evaluate the Ecumenical Challenges and Opportunities: Recognizing the theological division between *sola fide* and sacramental theology, this research examined how this debate affects modern ecumenical dialogues and Christian unity. It considered whether greater theological consensus can be achieved while maintaining doctrinal integrity.

Provide Practical Implications for Christian Faith and Practice: This research sought to highlight how the debate over faith and baptism affects believers' assurance of salvation, church membership, evangelism, and interdenominational relationships.

Ultimately, this research was geared toward contributing to the broader theological discourse on salvation, offering insights that help bridge doctrinal divides while reaffirming the foundational role of faith in Christian belief. The overall theme of this study illustrates the centrality of *sola fide* (faith alone) in the doctrine of salvation and its ongoing theological significance within Christian thought. At its core, this study demonstrates the enduring debate between Protestant, Catholic, and Orthodox traditions regarding the means to salvation—whether it is received by faith alone or mediated through sacramental acts such as baptism. The study underscores how *sola fide* was a defining principle of the Reformation and how it continues to shape Christian identity, doctrine, and ecumenical discussions today.

Additionally, the research illustrates how theological perspectives on justification influence Christian unity, church practices, and believers' assurance of salvation. It highlights both the divisions that persist in Christian theology and the opportunities for greater mutual understanding through scriptural engagement and ecumenical dialogue. Ultimately, this study reaffirms that faith is the cornerstone of salvation while recognizing the broader theological discourse that shapes the Christian experience across different traditions. Through careful analysis, it presents *sola fide* as not just a doctrinal position but a transformative reality that affects both individual faith and the collective witness of the Christian Church.

Recommendations

Based on the findings of this study on *sola fide* (faith alone) and its relationship to salvation and baptism, the following recommendations are proposed for future research, theological discourse, and ecumenical engagement:

1. Further Theological Investigation on Sola Fide and Baptism

Given the continued theological debate surrounding justification by faith alone and the role of baptism, future studies should explore more nuanced theological perspectives within different denominations. While this study primarily focused on Protestant, Catholic, and Orthodox traditions, further research could incorporate perspectives from Charismatic, Anabaptist, and emerging theological movements to provide a more comprehensive understanding of contemporary Christian beliefs.

2. Expanded Biblical Exegesis and Hermeneutical Analysis

Future research should include a deeper exegetical study of key biblical texts related to justification and baptism. While passages such as Ephesians 2:8-9, Romans 3:28, and John 3:16 were central to this study, additional scriptural analysis, including Old Testament foreshadowing and early church interpretations, could provide greater clarity on the role of faith and sacraments in salvation.

3. Broader Engagement with the Ecumenical Movement

As this study highlighted, *sola fide* remains a point of division in Christian theology, particularly between Protestant and sacramental traditions. Further research should explore how ecumenical dialogues have sought to reconcile differing views on justification and baptism. Examining documents such as the *Joint Declaration on the Doctrine of Justification* (1999) and other modern ecumenical agreements could provide insight into potential pathways for greater Christian unity.

4. Practical Implications for Church Practice and Teaching

Church leaders and theologians should consider how the doctrine of justification by faith alone is taught within their communities. Greater emphasis on doctrinal clarity can help mitigate misunderstandings regarding salvation and baptism. Future studies could explore how different churches implement *sola fide* in pastoral care, catechesis, and evangelism, especially in interdenominational contexts.

5. Recommendations for Future Research Methodology

If this study were to be repeated, greater care should be taken to expand the scope of theological sources, including more primary writings from early church fathers, Reformation-era theologians, and contemporary scholars from diverse Christian traditions. Additionally, more engagement with empirical research, such as surveys or interviews with church leaders and theologians, could offer valuable qualitative data on how *sola fide* and baptism are understood and practiced today.

In considering the use of a survey in this study, greater care should be taken in constructing survey statements to ensure clarity, precision, and alignment with the research objectives. More rigorous pre-testing and refinement of survey questions would enhance the validity of the data, allowing for more reliable correlations between theological beliefs, denominational affiliations, and perspectives on *sola fide* and baptism. The design of survey statements should incorporate both quantitative and qualitative elements, ensuring that responses capture not only doctrinal positions but also personal faith experiences and interpretative nuances.

Additionally, the study would have benefitted from a larger sample size to provide a more comprehensive analysis of Christian beliefs across different denominations, regions, and theological traditions. A broader and more diverse participant pool would allow for more accurate statistical comparisons between Protestant, Catholic, and Orthodox perspectives, yielding a clearer understanding of how justification by faith alone is perceived in various contexts. Expanding the research to include more international participants could also highlight cultural influences on the interpretation of *sola fide* and baptism.

Future research should also incorporate longitudinal studies or comparative analyses that track shifts in theological perspectives over time. This would help assess whether beliefs about justification and baptism evolve within Christian communities, particularly in light of modern ecumenical efforts and doctrinal discussions. Furthermore, integrating interviews or focus groups alongside survey methods could provide deeper qualitative insights, allowing researchers to explore the reasoning behind participants' theological positions. This mixed-methods approach would enhance the study's depth by capturing the complexity of individual faith journeys and doctrinal interpretations.

Future studies should emphasize more refined survey methodologies, expanded participant engagement, and multi-faceted data collection approaches to strengthen the research's ability to contribute meaningful insights to theological discourse on *sola fide* and baptism. In conclusion, the ongoing discussion on *sola fide* and baptism remains a vital theological issue with implications for Christian unity, doctrinal teaching, and personal faith. Future research should seek to bridge historical divisions while remaining faithful to biblical teachings on salvation by grace through faith.

Final Reflections

The doctrine of *sola fide*—justification by faith alone—has been one of the most defining and transformative theological convictions in Christian history. Rooted in Scripture and championed by the Reformers, this doctrine asserts that salvation is a gift of God's grace, received through faith in Jesus Christ, apart from human works or sacramental rites. While debates over the role of baptism and other sacraments continue to shape theological discourse, *sola fide* remains a foundational principle that influences Christian faith, practice, and the pursuit of unity among believers.

From a theological perspective, *sola fide* underscores the sufficiency of Christ's atoning work, which refers to the belief that Jesus Christ's sacrificial death on the cross fully accomplished the work of redemption, providing complete and final atonement for sin. This doctrine, central to *sola fide*, asserts that Christ's atonement alone is enough to reconcile sinners to God without the need for additional human effort, religious rituals, or sacramental works. It underscores the completeness of Christ's sacrifice, affirming that salvation depends entirely on God's grace rather than human merit. This has profound implications for Christian preaching and teaching, as it shifts the focus from religious performance to a personal and transformative faith in Christ. It reminds believers that righteousness is not something to be achieved through works but something freely given through faith, liberating individuals from the burden of trying to earn salvation.

Regarding Christian practice, sola fide shapes how believers approach discipleship, worship, and spiritual growth. While works are not the means of salvation, they remain an essential fruit of genuine faith. This doctrine compels Christians to live in gratitude and obedience, not to secure salvation but as a response to the grace they have received. Furthermore, it calls for a humility that acknowledges total dependence on God's mercy, fostering a Christ-centered life marked by love, service, and spiritual maturity.

From an ecumenical standpoint, *sola fide* continues to be a point of division and dialogue. While Protestant traditions uphold justification by faith alone, Catholic and Orthodox traditions integrate faith with sacraments, particularly baptism, as a means of receiving grace. Despite these theological differences, modern ecumenical efforts have sought common ground, emphasizing shared faith in Christ and the transformative power of grace. The challenge for Christian unity lies in balancing doctrinal convictions with a spirit of openness that encourages mutual understanding and respect among denominations.

In a contemporary context, *sola fide* remains relevant as it addresses the human tendency toward legalism and self-righteousness—the persistent human inclination toward legalism and self-righteousness, which continue to shape religious thought and practice in the contemporary world. Legalism refers to the belief that one's standing before God is dependent on strict adherence to rules, rituals, or moral efforts. Self-righteousness, in turn, emerges from the notion that personal virtue or religious performance earns divine approval. Both tendencies are deeply ingrained in human nature and have manifested throughout Christian history in various forms, often distorting the true essence of the gospel of grace.

In an age where religious pluralism and cultural shifts influence Christian identity, reaffirming faith alone as the cornerstone of salvation provides assurance and clarity to believers. It also serves as a corrective against both a works-based understanding of salvation and an antinomian disregard for holiness. An antinomian disregards holiness, believing that "under the gospel dispensation of grace, the moral law is of no use or obligation because faith alone is necessary to salvation" (*Merriam-Webster Dictionary*).

Ultimately, the doctrine of *sola fide* is not just a theological assertion but a transformative truth that affects how Christians view God, salvation, and their daily walk of faith. It affirms that salvation is secure not because of what believers do, but because of what Christ has done. As the Church continues to navigate theological debates and ecumenical conversations, the implications of *sola fide* remain central to the proclamation of the gospel and the lived experience of Christian faith.

References

Abel, A. I. (2024). Justification for eternal security of believers and impossibility of apostasy in Romans 8: 28-31. *African Journal of Religion, Philosophy and Culture, 5*(1), 25–46. ProQuest. http://nclive.org/cgi-bin/nclsm?url=http://search.proquest.com/scholarly-journals/justification-eternal-security-believers/docview/3100427284/se-2, doi:https://doi.org/10.31920/2634-7644/2024/v5n1a2.

Augustine. *The city of God* (H. Bettenson, Trans.). Penguin Classics, 2003.

Barrett, Matthew P. V. (2019). *Sola fide: The reformed doctrine of justification.* Crossway.

Beasley-Murray, G. R. (1962). *Baptism in the New Testament.* Wm. B. Eerdmans Publishing.

Beza, T., Polanus, A., & Turrentin, F. (2023). *Justification by faith alone* (C. B. Carmichael, Trans.). Reformation Heritage Books.

Calvin, J. (2006). *Institutes of the Christian religion.* (H. Beveridge, Trans.). Hendrickson Publishers.

Calvin, J. (2008). *Institutes of the Christian religion.* (H. Beveridge, Trans.). Hendrickson Publishers.

Captivating History. (2021). *The reformation: A captivating guide to the religious revolution sparked by Martin Luther and its impact on Christianity and the Western Church.* Vicelane.

Catechism of the Catholic Church. 2nd ed., Libreria Editrice Vaticana, 1997.

Catechism of the Catholic Church. 2nd ed., Libreria Editrice Vaticana, 2000.

Ferguson, E. (2009). *Baptism in the early church: History, theology, and liturgy in the first five centuries.* Eerdmans.

Gates, H. L., Jr. (2021). *The Black church: This is our story, this is our song.* Penguin Press.

George, T. (2004). The role of justification by faith in the Reformation and today. *Southern Baptist Journal of Theology, 8*(3), 4-19.

González, J. L. (2010). *The story of Christianity, Volume 1: The early church to the dawn of the Reformation.* HarperOne.

Grudem, W. (1994). *Systematic theology: An introduction to biblical doctrine.* Zondervan Academic.

Grudem, W. (2020). *Systematic theology: An introduction to biblical doctrine* (2nd ed.). Zondervan Academic.

Heinze, R. W. (2005). *Reform and conflict: From the medieval world to the wars of religion* (vol. 4). Baker Books.

Horsley, R. A. (2005). *Christian origins* (Vol. 1). *A people's history of Christianity.* Fortress Press.

Ingolfsland, D. (2022). *Perspectives on Paul: Five views.* (Vol. 65). Evangelical Theological Society. Lynchburg.

Johnson, G. L. W. (2007). *By faith alone: Answering the challenges to the doctrine of justification.* Crossway.

Kelly, J. N. D. (1978). *Early Christian doctrines.* Harper & Row.

Küng, H. (1994). *Great Christian thinkers.* Continuum.

Luther, M. (1963). *Three treatises* (W. A. Lambert & H. J. Grimm). Fortress Press.

Luther, M. (1970). *The Babylonian captivity of the church, 1520*. In A. T. W. Steinhaeuser (Trans.), *Three treatises*. Fortress Press.

MacArthur, J. (1995). *The gospel according to Jesus: What Is authentic faith?* Zondervan.

MacCulloch, D. (2010). *Christianity: The first three thousand years*. Penguin Books.

McGrath, A. E. (1998). *Iustitia Dei: A history of the Christian doctrine of justification* (3rd ed.). Cambridge University Press.

McGrath, A. E. (2017). *Christian theology: An introduction* (6th ed.,). Wiley-Blackwell.

McGrath, A. E. (2021). *Reformation thought: An introduction* (5th ed.). Wiley-Blackwell.

Merriam-Webster. (n.d.). Antinomian. In *Merriam-Webster.com dictionary*. Retrieved Feb 19, 2025, from https://www.merriam-webster.com/dictionary/antinomian.

O'Malley, J. W. (2008). Baptism and the early church: A historical perspective. *Theological Studies, 69*(4), 850-872.

Piper, J. (2007). *The future of justification: A response to N. T. Wright*. Crossway.

Plant, T. R. (2024). Shinjin, faith, and sacramental metaphysics. *Buddhist - Christian Studies, 44*, 41-55. *ProQuest*, http://nclive.org/cgi-bin/nclsm?url=http://search.proquest.com/scholarly-journals/shinjin-faith-sacramental-metaphysics/docview/3118074852/se-2.

Ryrie, A. (2017). *Protestants: The faith that made the modern world.* Viking.

Schreiner, T. R. (2015). *Faith alone: The doctrine of justification: What the Reformers taught...and why it still matters.* Zondervan Academic.

Schreiner, T. R., & Shawn D. W. (Eds.). (2006). *Believer's baptism: Sign of the new covenant in Christ.* B&H Academic.

Sproul, R. C. (1995). *Faith alone: The evangelical doctrine of justification.* Baker Books.

Sproul, R. C. (2014). *Faith alone: The evangelical doctrine of justification.* Baker Books.

Sproul, R. C., (Ed.). (1997). *Justification by faith alone: Affirming the doctrine by which the church and the individual stands or falls.* Soli Deo Gloria Publications.

The Holy Bible, English Standard Version. (2001). Crossway.

The Holy Bible, King James Version. (2017). Nelson.

The Holy Bible, New International Version. (2011). Zondervan.

Trueman, C. (2012). Luther on faith and works: Understanding justification in the reformation. *Westminster Theological Journal, 74*(2), 247-265.

Trueman, C. R. (2017). *Grace alone: Salvation as a gift of God: What the Reformers taught...and why it still matters.* Zondervan Academic.

Waters, G. P. (2004). *The doctrine of justification: What the Reformers taught...and why it still matters.* Reformation Trust Publishing.

Westminster Assembly. (2003). *The Westminster Confession of Faith.* Free Presbyterian Publications.

Wilson, A. N. (1997). *Paul: The mind of the Apostle.* W. W. Norton & Company.

World Council of Churches. (1982). *Baptism, Eucharist, and Ministry (BEM) document. Faith and Order Paper No. 111.*

Wright, N. T. (2008). *Surprised by hope: Rethinking Heaven, the Resurrection, and the mission of the Church.* HarperOne.

Wright, N. T. (2013). *Paul and the faithfulness of God.* Fortress Press.